Card...

& the Birth of Ca... ...ocial Teaching

by
Russell Sparkes

*All booklets are published thanks to the
generous support of the members of the
Catholic Truth Society*

CATHOLIC TRUTH SOCIETY
PUBLISHERS TO THE HOLY SEE

Contents

Thoughts and words 3

One of the greatest men of his age 5

The forgotten Victorian 8

Early life and character 12

The path to Rome 21

Prayer and turbulence 29

The champion of infallibility 40

The Father of Catholic Social Teaching 49

Education of the poor 53

Calling for a change of policy in Ireland 56

Manning's role in the Great Dock Strike 66

'The Eternal Priesthood' 69

Manning's influence on the Church 71

The public's depth of affection 74

Dedication
To my daughter Catherine - simply for being Cate.

Thoughts and words

'The mind of Christ must be transfused into our own. There must be somewhat of the same intense love of perishing sinners, of the same patient endurance of moral evil, and unwearied striving to bring the impenitent to God... What a mission, Brethren, is ours!' *Manning*, 1835.

'You should ha' seen him in Church. He were a wonderful Churchman. He looked like an Archangel when he prayed.' *Sussex Countryman.* 1877.

'What can be more formidable than to stand between the living and the dead, charged with the priestly office, to give account for the souls committed to our trust? The Fathers call it an office which angels fear to bear.' *Manning* 1883.

'The intensity of his nature... could not be doubted by anyone who had seen him in Church or at prayer... I could see a word written on the forehead of that man, and that word is *sacerdos*.' *Aubrey de Vere* 1897.

'From my plane of thought and life, I can only look at him (Manning) as a man looks at the stars.'

Gladstone 1896

'In close contact with him one felt that he was always living in the presence of an unseen power... as its simple and humble messenger... nothing so impressive, so faith-inspiring has ever met my eyes as the sight of this noble old Englishman in his threadbare cassock kneeling before the altar of his bare chapel.' *Bodley* 1912.

One of the greatest men of his age

The Victorian age was a period that produced many great
men and women. Hilaire Belloc described Cardinal
Manning, whom he knew well as a young man, as the
greatest of them all. Many contemporaries shared that
opinion. Nor was admiration of Manning limited to the
rich and famous. On the contrary. After Manning's death
in 1892 the crowds thronged his funeral procession
through the streets of London in a way that had been seen
only once before for the funeral of the Duke of
Wellington forty years earlier.

Destroying visceral anti-Catholicism

Just one of Manning's many achievements was the ending
of London's previously well deserved reputation for fear
and hatred of Catholicism. The city had been one of the
original centres of the Reformation in the 1520s, and it
retained its fear and distrust of the Catholic Church for
hundreds of years. In the 1678 the mob terrorized the city
in the 'Popish Plot' disturbances, while just over a
hundred years later London was rocked by the
'No-Popery' Gordon riots. Indeed, when the Catholic
hierarchy was re-established in 1850 the government

feared that this could lead yet again to anti-Catholic riots in London.

Yet a mere forty years later this visceral anti-Catholicism had been destroyed, due in large part by Manning's selfless devotion to the poor. Right from the beginning of his ministry he warned employers of the need to treat workers decently and actively campaigned for better working conditions and housing for the poor, particularly in London. Indeed, when the great Dock Strike of 1889 threatened to paralyse Victorian Britain, it was the Cardinal, the only authority figure trusted by dock workers, who was able to end it. He was also the main inspirational force behind the flourishing of Catholic Social Teaching in the last part of the nineteenth century culminating in the great social encyclical *Rerum Novarum*[1] in 1891.

Conversion and profundity

Born an Anglican, Manning became an Archdeacon, a senior figure in the Church of England. After much personal agonising he decided in 1851 that he was morally obliged to be received into the Catholic Church, despite the huge blow that this would cause to family and friends. Manning was also noted for his great personal austerity and as a profound spiritual counsellor.

Defining 'Infallibility' and strengthening the Church

He also played a crucial role in the definition of 'Infallibility' at the first Vatican Council of 1869-70. Indeed, the English Catholic Church as we know it today is largely Manning's creation. He was the second Archbishop of Westminster, a post he held for an astonishing 27 years. During this time Manning worked tirelessly to support and teach the Catholic faithful at a time when they were growing rapidly in number. He encouraged the creation of new Catholic schools, opened seminaries to train new priests, and built new churches.

The forgotten Victorian

Yet Manning's achievements, and indeed his name, are largely forgotten today. This is strange as biographies of the famous Victorians continue to pour off the press. Over ten books have been published about Florence Nightingale in the last ten years alone, even more has been written about Newman; on Manning, nothing. The last new biography about the great Cardinal was by Robert Gray[2] twenty five years ago!

The malice of his biographer Purcell

Why he is so little known? Two reasons I think. The first is that Manning's reputation was deliberately savaged shortly after his death through the malice of his biographer Purcell, an Irish journalist who was known to have a grudge against him. When Manning died in 1892 his appointed biographer J.C. Bodley was abroad. Immediately Purcell asked to see his papers and proceeded to cart many of them off in a van without any legal right to do so. He then dashed out a large, inaccurate and heavily biased biography. As Robert Gray puts it:

'The portrait he drew… was of an ecclesiastic consumed by ambition and the will to dominate, prepared to gain his ends by any means, however unscrupulous… To this reader it seems incontestable that the whole work is pervaded by malice.'[3]

In his biography Purcell quite deliberately painted a distorted picture of Manning as a cold manipulative character who lacked normal emotion but was driven by ambition. Manning expert David Newsome agrees about Purcell's bias:

'The hostile animus of the author is exhibited by the way in which he consistently puts the worst interpretation upon Manning's actions, reflections, and motives… Purcell accuses him of being the victim of ruthless ambition, of exhibiting calculated duplicity in his last years within the Anglican Church.'[4]

To my mind what Purcell did was unspeakable. He took Manning's private spiritual journals, in which throughout his life Manning had written down his struggles and determination to live his life to the highest possible spiritual standards, and totally distorted them to depict a monster. I am sure that Manning tried to live a saint-like life of deep spirituality and asceticism, and it was criminal of Purcell to deliberately distort extracts from these journals in order to show Manning as a man eaten up with pride. The opposite was true; as a true ascetic Manning constantly strove to look at himself in the least flattering light, and his personal reflections show how he ruthlessly exposed and fought against his weaknesses such as pride and the desire to have his own way.

Some twenty five years later, when Lytton Strachey was looking for a theme to mock the Victorian period, Purcell's biography inspired him to write a series of four essays on leading Victorians called *Eminent Victorians:* Florence Nightingale, General Gordon, Thomas Arnold of Rugby School, and of course Cardinal Manning. Indeed, the essay on Manning is by far the longest in the book. As Newsome states:

> 'In fact, it was through reading Purcell's biography in a moment of boredom, that Strachey conceived the idea of writing the book… What made Strachey's caricature so unpardonable was that in using Purcell he dredged up charges (from other sources) that he must have known were untrue.'[5]

The spirit of Vatican I

There is a second reason why, I believe, Manning has been forgotten. It has been said that Manning's strict dogmatism and emphasis on the authority of the *magisterium* was in the spirit of Vatican I, whereas Newman's more individual faith with its greater role for the laity was in the spirit of Vatican II. In that case it is no surprise that as Newman's reputation has risen over the last sixty years, Manning's has fallen.

However, we live in a period when, as Manning predicted long ago, the Church is coming under increasing attack from secular authorities, curiously enough often in the name of 'tolerance'. I therefore hope that this CTS booklet will help re-establish the truth about Manning, a giant figure in the 'Second Spring' of English Catholicism.

Early life and character

Henry Edward Manning was born on the 15th July 1808, the youngest child of the family. He was born into a prosperous background, as his father, William Manning, was a rich sugar trader. The family religion was 'High and Dry' Anglicanism, with regular attendance at fairly formal Church of England services.

The Manning and Wilberforce families

However, the Evangelical revival of the second half of the 18th century, started by John Wesley, had led to a return to classic Protestant doctrines of an individual encounter with God directly through the Scriptures. One of the most important of these Evangelicals was William Wilberforce, a founder member of the Campaign Against the Slave Trade in 1787. There was a strong Evangelical influence upon the young Henry Manning, as it was his mother's faith, while there were also links between the Manning and Wilberforce families.

Good-looking with a very strong personality

As a boy he was notable for two things: being physically good-looking, and for having a very strong personality. Throughout his adult life Manning was well aware that he was a man of great practical talents: shrewd, determined, practical, with a capacity for immense hard work and a powerful ability to influence others. He was an intense, often 'driven' man with a strong sense of duty. While he was attracted to worldly success, his spiritual journals show how he continually fought against these temptations.

A 'stiff upper lip'

He would have made a great diplomat; calm, collected, composed, he could listen quietly to others whilst giving away little of what he really believed. This is why some people thought he was duplicitous. I am sure that Manning himself thought he was simply doing his best to do his duty by keeping control of a difficult situation. He could seem aloof, but this reflected the classic Victorian belief that a gentleman kept his emotions under control and did not reveal them- what would later be called a 'stiff upper lip.'

A tendency to sniff

Like most affluent children of the period, Manning was educated by private tutors before being sent in 1822 aged fourteen to Harrow, one of the great public schools of England. He also suffered severe asthma attacks, which bothered him for the rest of his life. (Indeed, his asthma led him to have a tendency to sniff, sometimes just expressing irritation or annoyance. Years later, the Cardinal's sniff could spread terror among the younger clergy of the diocese.)

Wary of intimacy

In 1826 he heard news that his sister Harriet, his only close family member was seriously ill; dashing home from school, he arrived to find her dying. He wrote: 'Her death was a great loss to me and left me alone; the others being so much older as to be no companions to me'. Indeed, I think that Harriet's sudden death traumatized the boy and made him wary of intimacy with other people, a personality trait that became overwhelming after another catastrophic death eleven years later.

The best public speaker in Oxford

In the autumn of 1827 Manning went up to study at Balliol College, Oxford, and in the spring of 1829 he started to attend the newly opened Oxford Union, the university debating society. To general surprise he quickly supplanted the Union's established favorites such as William Gladstone, with whom he became close friends to become the best public speaker in Oxford. Later that year he was elected President of the Oxford Union.

Political ambitions

From his youth Manning had intended to enter the Church of England. However, his success in the Oxford

Union turned his head towards politics, and in 1829-1830 he started to study avidly political theory and economics. However, events were to frustrate these plans. After the end of the Napoleonic Wars in 1815 the economy fell into a bitter and prolonged depression. This slump put great pressure on William Manning's business, which failed in 1831.

Giving up politics at the dictate of reason and conscience

In this period politics was dominated by rich aristocratic families; with the loss of the family's fortune Manning's dreams of a political career were more or less over. When he left Oxford in the winter of 1830 his family urged him to go into business where they retained good contacts, but he felt an insistent religious calling:

'This feeling that God was calling me worked continually. I told no one. I could not lay it. Every day it grew upon me and I found myself face to face with this choice: to leave all that I was attracted to, and to take up all that I shrunk from. If ever I made a choice in my life in which my superior will controlled my inferior will, it was when I gave up all the desires, hopes and aspirations after public life at the dictate of my reason and my conscience.'

Becoming a deacon

In 1832 he was elected a Fellow of Merton College, where he devoured the College Library of religious works. In December 1832 he became a deacon, the first step towards Anglican priesthood. The evidence suggests that Manning intended to spend several years at Merton, reading theology and pondering his future. But events were about to change his life for ever.

In late 1832 John Sargent, the Rector of Lavington and Graffham, two small villages near Chichester in Sussex, decided that he needed a curate to help him out. Sargent was a highly respected and wealthy Evangelical whose family owned the Estate of East Lavington, and had the right to appoint the vicar of the parish. The Sargent and Wilberforce families were close. John Sargent's wife Mary was a cousin of William Wilberforce, while in 1829 Samuel Wilberforce married Emily Sargent, John's eldest daughter. She was one of his four daughters, all generally described as beautiful with fair hair and a rosy complexion.

Eighteen years at Lavington

In January 1833 Manning went to Lavington for what he thought would be a brief, temporary visit, but he was to stay for 18 years. He arrived in Lavington on the 3rd January 1833, and by Easter he was engaged to marry Caroline, then aged 21. Virtually nothing is known of the marriage. However, what we do know indicates that they were very happy and devoted to each other.

Married by Samuel Wilberforce

However, there was a dark cloud over the Sargent household; the girls' rosy complexion was a sign of the 'consumption' or tuberculosis that was to kill most of them at relatively young age. Events now moved quickly for Manning. The Rector, a healthy man in the prime of life, suddenly caught pneumonia and died quite unexpectedly on 3 May 1833. His mother decided to use her power of appointment to make Manning the new Rector. On 9 June he was therefore ordained priest by Bishop Maltby of Chichester. As soon as a respectable six months period of mourning was over, Caroline and Manning were married by her brother in law Samuel Wilberforce on November 7th. Whilst on honeymoon Manning wrote to her mother Mary a letter which is highly suggestive that Caroline's health was already suffering:

> 'She bore the journey surprisingly well, and has been more like herself, with the vigour, and activity she used to show, than I have seen for many, many months.'

The life of a country parson

When they returned home Manning settled into the life of a country parson. On becoming Rector he visited all the houses in the parish. Lord Chichester described him as 'the most exemplary clergyman he had ever known, alike for his parochial zeal and his personal holiness.' He was well known for wandering around the parish on foot, visiting the poor and sick, and for his intense spirituality at prayer. Nevertheless, although he tried hard to get to know the local people and played cricket with them, he lacked the common touch.

Manning's wife dies of consumption

In July 1835 Manning's sermon in Chichester Cathedral, on *The English Church*, was published to national acclaim, and he contributed No 58 of the *Tracts for the Times* in 1837. However, by now his personal life was collapsing. In February 1837 he wrote to Newman:

'My wife has been, and still is in a state of the most alarming danger... the one who was in an earthly way all things to me seems to be bidden to an early rest.'

By now she was exhibiting the bloody cough symptomatic of the final stages of consumption. She finally died on 24th July 1837, aged only 25. Manning's refusal to talk about it was later seized upon by his critics. As Robert Gray notes:

'There has been no more vicious, but unfortunately no more enduring, calumny against Manning than Lytton Strachey's snide insinuation that he came to regard

Caroline's death as a deliverance from an alliance that would otherwise have held him back from the Catholic priesthood. For many people it is the sole thing that they remember about Manning. Strachey deliberately perverted his sources to achieve this libel.'[6]

His longing for his dead wife was 'like a furnace'

Caroline's mother, Mary Sargent later wrote that her daughter's dying words to her were: 'I am sure Mama you will do all you can to take care of Henry', and she remained always supportive of him. Manning forced himself to show little apparent emotion, and he tried to numb the pain through intensive work. Nevertheless, he told Samuel Wilberforce after the burial that his longing for his dead wife was, 'like a furnace', while on the second anniversary of Caroline's death Mary Sargent discovered him in 'quite an agony of grief.' Fr James Pereiro believes that this event forced him in on himself:

'Manning remained a deeply emotional person throughout his life. But he didn't let much out, fearing that he could easily lose control of his feelings. Although he was very close to other women, particularly from his own family, finding great support in them, none of this ever came close to what he had experienced with Caroline.'[7]

No gravestone

Fifty years later the aged Archbishop came back to visit Lavington, which had been inherited in 1841 by the Wilberforce family. For several minutes Manning stood silently beside the unmarked grave of Caroline. When her nephew Reginald Wilberforce dared to ask asked him why there was no gravestone, the reply came back: 'Because I could not put on it the inscription that I should have wished.'

Every year he received a rose from her grave

There was a touching modern footnote to this story. In 1960, when the Oxford academic David Newsome was researching Manning's life, a very old lady came to see him. She told him that some seventy years before, as a young girl, her father Reginald Wilberforce had sent her every year on the anniversary of Caroline's death to London to give a rose from her grave to the Cardinal. The old man would cherish it and then burst into tears. There was never any question of him remarrying. In 1890 he wrote in his journal that:

'I have lived as a widower without ever wavering in the purpose of living and dying as I am now'.

The path to Rome

From this time on Manning became noted for his great personal austerity and as a profound spiritual counsellor. In 1837 he was appointed Rural Dean, often a sinecure, but not for him. In 1840 his diligence was rewarded when he was appointed Archdeacon, the most senior clerical position below that of a bishop.

Inner tension and uncertainty

When he threw himself into his work after Caroline's death, the temper of Manning's mind demanded that this should have a systematic and well-grounded basis. Unfortunately for Manning, the more he read and thought about theology, the less, rather than the more, secure the spiritual foundations of his life turned out to be. Indeed, the next fourteen years until he was received into the Catholic Church in 1851 were marked by inner tension and uncertainty and even a sense of drift, most unusual for this most purposeful of men.

From an Evangelical to a more Catholic understanding

Manning continued studying to deepen his spiritual knowledge. His initial views were those of the

Evangelical wing of the Church of England- doubtful of formal liturgy and the sacraments. However, as he read seventeenth century writers like Hooker and Jeremy Taylor, he moved from an Evangelical to a more Catholic understanding of the real presence of Christ in the Eucharist. One thing that struck him particularly forcibly when he became a parish priest was how to justify his priestly authority, especially among the poor:

> 'The first question that rose to my mind was, "What right have you to be teaching, admonishing, reforming, rebuking others? By what authority do you lift the latch of a poor man's door and enter and sit down and begin to instruct or correct him? if not a messenger sent from God, I was an intruder and impertinent.'

The Tractarian movement

This was an extremely unusual way of thinking at a time when the Church of England was regarded as a key component of maintaining the established social order. It was dominated by the State, and 'latitudinarian', or lax, on doctrinal matters. It was also a period when the Oxford Movement, or 'Tractarians', powerfully advocated a more Catholic spirit in the Church of England. Their leader was John Henry Newman, whose first 'Tract for the Times' had appeared in September 1833. The Tractarian movement was quite a radical, innovative force in the Church of England, combining as it did the deep personal faith and enthusiasm of the Evangelicals with the ecclesiastical and sacramental principles of the High Church. However, their advocacy of Catholic practices with the Anglican Church was always controversial, as they were always a small if vocal minority within the Church of England. Purcell and Strachey's accusation that Manning constantly courted promotion is obvious nonsense, as his Tractarian sympathies actually impeded them!

The rule of faith – a sermon

In 1838 Manning gave a sermon setting out one of the themes that would occupy him for the rest of his life, i.e. that the national interest not only required the education of the poor (extremely prescient for the time) but that the moral health of the country required it to be provided by the Church and not by the State. In June 1838 he came to national prominence with a sermon published under the title, *The Rule of Faith*. His aim was:

'Not to enquire what are the specific *doctrines* of the Gospel, but what is the rule by which we may ascertain them'.

Indeed, until 1851 the idea of establishing a 'rule of faith' dominated Manning's thinking. His intense nature required certainty of belief, which he thought he found in the tradition of the Church Fathers going back to the Apostles. He argued that Vincentius' phrase *'quod semper, quod ubique, quod ab omnibus'*, ('what was always believed by everybody and everywhere'), represented the belief of the one universal Christian church and was therefore certain or infallible.

'The Unity of the Church' – a major book

In 1842 Manning published his first major book on theology, dedicated to his great friend Gladstone, entitled *The Unity of the Church*. It argued that the Christian Church was divided into three valid branches: Orthodox, Roman Catholic, and Anglican, and put forward the case that it was fidelity to the simple faith of the Apostles which enabled the Church to remain united despite its apparent divisions. In it he stressed the essential teaching role of the Church, without which individual study of the Bible risked turning into subjectivity: 'Man has a tendency to put subjective opinion in the place of objective truth.' It was generally recognized at the time as a major piece of work.

A candidate for the highest offices in the Church of England

As the 1840s progressed Manning's obvious ability meant that he was a candidate for the highest offices in the Church of England. In 1844 the Anglican priest Allies wrote: 'Manning (is) the best spiritual guide we have'.

The formidable Bishop of Exeter declared: 'Manning in the Church, Gladstone in the State, and Hope in the Law... No power on earth can keep Manning from the Bench (of Bishops).' However, Manning was about to get an enormous shock.

Newman converts and Manning becomes uncertain

Newman, the charismatic preacher and leader of the Oxford Movement, had increasingly come to doubt his vision of the Church of England as a *via media*. In October 1843 he wrote in confidence to a shocked and horrified Manning that he had lost faith in the Church of England and was likely to become a Roman Catholic, although this did not actually happen until October 1845.

In 1845 Newman published his acclaimed *Essay on Development*, which justified his move to Rome by analysing the process of theological development. Gladstone asked Manning to write a rebuttal of this. However, the more he studied it, and the issues it raised, the more uncertain he became:

'It opened my eyes to one fact, namely that I had laid down only half the subject. I had found *the Rule*, but not *the Judge*. It was evident that to put Scripture and Antiquity into the hands of the individual is as much private judgement as to put Scripture alone... the perpetuity of the Faith must have a higher basis than the individual or collective intellect of the Church...

The Universal Church of the first 700 years believed in divine, infallible guidance in its office... What does Reason say but that the *certitude* of revelation to succeeding ages demands a perpetual provision from error?.'

Spiritual development

For the next six years this normally determined and purposeful man was drifting. The more he studied Catholic theology, the stronger its case seemed to him, particularly its answer to the question of 'the rule of faith'. As Pereiro has noted in his study of Manning's spiritual development:

'Manning's mind had a strong inclination, and an evident power for synthesis. He may have preached his sermons on apostolic succession and the rule of faith urged by the questions raised by his pastoral ministry... however, he was always working the knowledge he acquired into a general scheme, always looking for the connections between ideas, trying to integrate principles and concepts into a coherent vision of reality.'[8]

Rejection of promotion and bitter spiritual anguish

To add to his problems there were few people he could discuss them with. As an Anglican Archdeacon he was obliged to publicly uphold the doctrines of the Church of

England. In December 1845 Manning was offered the post of Sub-Almoner to the Archbishop of York, generally recognized as a route to the highest offices in the Anglican Church. To general surprise Manning turned it down: 'People were expecting and predicting all things for me, and I was making them impossible'. Events now moved quickly. He developed a facial tic under the immense strain of being seen as the new leader of the Tractarians, just as his own confidence in their beliefs was failing. In February 1847 his health totally collapsed for four months. Coughing up blood he feared he was dying from consumption, like Caroline ten years earlier. His journals written whilst confined to bed in this period set out bitter spiritual anguish.

A visit to Newman and a sign in Milan

When he recovered in July he visited Rome where Newman did not recognize him as his face was so withered by illness. On his way back home Manning visited the shrine of St Charles Borromeo in Milan, and took what he felt was a sign:

'I was thinking in prayer, if only I could know that St Charles, who represents the Council of Trent, was right and we wrong. The Deacon was singing the Gospel, and the last words, *et erit unum ovile et unus pastor,* (and there will be one flock and one shepherd) came upon me, as if I had never heard them before.'

Archdeacon Manning resigns – the last straw

A series of political issues also undermined the Tractarian view of the Church of England as independent. The last straw occurred in November 1850 following the restoration of the Catholic hierarchy in England. As Archdeacon Manning was required to lead a meeting in Chichester Cathedral repudiating the claims of the newly appointed Cardinal Wiseman. Manning called the meeting to order, but resigned during it.

'My old friend the Dean was crying, and many others. So we ended and parted. It was our last meeting and the end of my work in the Church of England.'

Received into the Catholic faith

He left Lavington for good on 3rd Dec 1850 and moved to live with his sister in London. Poignantly, it was only a week after the reconsecration of East Lavington church, which he had spent years rebuilding. On the 6 April 1851 he was received into the Catholic Faith in London, together with Gladstone's friend, the lawyer James Hope.

Gladstone felt as if Manning had 'murdered my mother'

It was generally accepted that a great future in the Church of England had been thrown away. Gladstone was horrified by the news, saying that he felt as if Manning had 'murdered my mother!', and never forgave him.

Prayer and turbulence

After his reception into the Catholic Church Manning planned to live quietly as a layman for at least a year to take stock of his life. However, these plans were to be frustrated as he was just the sort of man Cardinal Wiseman, the newly arrived head of the Catholic Church, desperately needed. Manning was therefore persuaded to enter the priesthood, on Trinity Sunday 14 June 1851. Wiseman told him:

> 'I look upon you as one of the first fruits of the restoration of the hierarchy by our Holy Father Pius IX. Go forth, my son, and bring your brethren and fellow countrymen into the one true fold of Christ.'

Post Reformation persecution

The Catholic Church he joined was very different from the one we know now. For about 250 years after the Reformation Catholics faced intense persecution. Both laity and priests risked execution for their beliefs, the confiscation of their property, as well as being banned from political life, the legal profession, or attending the universities.

The Vatican treats England as a missionary province

By the late eighteenth century the Catholic Church had almost been wiped out, with Edmund Burke calculating in 1780 that there were only 70,000 Catholics left in the whole of the country, principally concentrated in isolated valleys in the north of England. They had only survived because of the support provided by Catholic local aristocratic families; there were no churches, only chapels attached to country houses. Their attitude to life was to keep a rigidly low profile; priests did not wear clerical garb, and were addressed as 'Mister', not 'Father'. Their faith was also antiquated, as many devotional practices such as the Exposition of the Blessed Sacrament were unknown. The conventional diocesan structure had also been wiped out. From 1623 the Vatican administered England as a missionary province, run by the Congregation of Propaganda in Rome. Priests were normally provided by regular orders, principally Jesuits.

A highly introverted community without structure

Thus English Catholicism in the early nineteenth century was essentially a highly introverted community, dominated by proudly 'Old Catholic' aristocratic families that totally lacked the modern parish and diocesan structure. This presented big problems to Wiseman when he tried to restore normal ecclesiastical authority in 1851, and it explains the bitter in-fighting which sadly so bedevilled the next thirty years or so. One big problem was that members of the religious orders were responsible to their own superiors, not to the local bishop. (The issue was not finally resolved until 1881, when persistent campaigning by the then Cardinal Manning resulted in the Papal bull *Romanos Pontifices*. This ruled that the regular orders had to get the bishop's prior consent before they could open any new school or religious community in a diocese.)

Popular prejudice

The intense anti-Catholic propaganda of the Reformation period had also left its mark in a strong popular prejudice of 'No-Popery'. This burst forth again when the English Catholic hierarchy was finally restored on 29th September 1850. *The Times* was typical:

'The Pope and his advisers have mistaken our complete tolerance for indifference to their designs; they have mistaken the renovated zeal of the Church in this country for a return to Romish bondage.'

England's first census

England's first census, held in 1851, recorded a Catholic population of just over 250,000. However, this missed a massive influx of Irish people who had recently immigrated to flee the horrors of the Great Famine. Most historians believe that the true number in 1851 was probably around 700,000: 100,000 Old Catholics; 100,000 Catholics living in the new industrial cities in Lancashire and Yorkshire, and 500,000 desperately poor Irish, generally living in the slums of big cities: London, Liverpool, Manchester, and Birmingham.

Priestly formation needed to be centralised

When the French Revolution launched a massive attack on the Catholic Church in France from 1790 onwards, the Vatican responded by reasserting the central authority of the Pope, a movement generally called 'ultramontanism'. Increased Papal authority was generally welcomed outside England, but the Old Catholics clung to their independent or 'Liberal Catholic' traditions. Cardinal Wiseman was utterly convinced that the English Church had to be built on ultramontane lines to bring it into line with the Church elsewhere. Chapels located in isolated valleys in the North of England were of little help to the newly arrived poor Irish, who needed the construction of churches on a large scale and the rapid expansion of priestly formation, which could only be done in a centralised way.

Old Catholic resistance and poor Irish need

However, the vast majority of the clergy he inherited were, hardly surprisingly, from an Old Catholic background, and bitterly resistant to his proposed changes and new 'Italianate' devotions. On the other hand the poor

Irish welcomed the rousing ritual he brought with him; for them the local Catholic Church was their only social centre in a life of hard labour and slum dwelling. In 1850 there were 587 Catholic churches in England & Wales, and 788 clergy. By 1900 there were 1,529 churches and 2,812 clergy. The 700,000 Catholics of 1851 became 1,300,000 by 1901. In ecclesiastical historian Sheridan Gilley's words:

'It was however, arguably the Ultramontanization of the Church that made it a success, as the new gaudy chapels with their altars and statues and smell of incense and melted beeswax projected a sense of the sacred.'[9]

Wiseman advocates ritualism and ultramonatism

Wiseman himself was a distinguished scholar and founder of the *Dublin Review*, to which he was a regular contributor, a good judge of people, and politically aware. He liked exuberant ritual and hosting fine dinners, but he also made a point of visiting the poor in the slums of London. Yet both the ritualism and the ultramontanism were deeply unpopular with the Old Catholic laity. As Edward Norman put it:

'They sensed that his clericalism would exalt the priesthood and depress the laity to the point at which they would lose all influence. Wiseman, for his part, saw the universal authority of papal monarchy as an essential barrier against the indifferentism and infidelity of the age, and although he was open to modern scholarship, as he understood it, he saw English Protestantism all round him sinking into liberalism and ultimate scepticism.'[10]

Wiseman seizes on Manning's skills

Wiseman also had one major weakness- he was poor at administration. Given this weakness, and the lack of domestic support for his ultramontane views, it must have seemed providential to Wiseman when Manning, a brilliant administrator and committed ultramontane himself, turned up a few months after his own arrival in England. Manning's rapid rise through the ranks of the Church in the next few years may seem surprising at first sight given the widespread suspicion of converts. However, it is not when his beliefs and skills are taken into account.

Wiseman sent him to Rome to study

After ordination Wiseman sent him to Rome to study at the *Accademia Ecclesiastica*, generally regarded as a place for future cardinals. Manning had become fluent in Italian in his youth- a huge advantage when he was in Rome. In the autumn of 1851 Manning went to Rome along with Aubrey de Vere.

The loss of Caroline's letters severs 'all bonds to earth'

However, when they stopped at Avignon disaster struck, as a small black bag contained Caroline's letters was stolen. They were never recovered. De Vere wrote:

> 'At the first moment after the discovery of the loss the expression of grief in his face and voice was such as I have seldom witnessed. He spoke little; and when I was beginning to speak, he laid his hand upon my arm, and said, "Say nothing! I can just endure it when I keep perfectly silent." …We met again at Rome. He met my enquiries with a brief reply. "No; the loss was probably necessary- necessary to sever all bonds to earth"'.

The first ever synod of the Catholic bishops

When he reached Rome he quickly established a close rapport with the Pope. Travelling back in the summer of 1852 he met a 20 year old candidate for the priesthood, Herbert Vaughn, who after initial wariness of 'the old parson' became devoted to him. 1852 was also the year of the first ever synod of the Catholic bishops held at Oscott, near Birmingham. Wiseman invited both Manning and Newman to give prominent sermons, the latter declaring:

> 'It is the coming in of a Second Spring; it is a restoration in the moral world.'

A mission to raise the status of the secular clergy

When Manning finished his studies in Rome in September 1854 the Pope asked him to stay at Rome and offered him the post of Papal Chamberlain. However, he came back to fulfil Wiseman's idea that the London poor could only be truly helped by raising the status of the secular clergy among them. Wiseman had previously asked the regular orders such as the Jesuits to help him do this, but they had declined. In 1853 Manning got a handwritten note at the Accademia from Wiseman asking him to return to England. Wiseman wanted 'an Oratory with external action'; secular clergy whose spiritual life was sanctified by a life lived in community.

Father Superior of the Oblates

Manning totally agreed and used the model of the Oblates found by St Charles Borromeo in Milan three hundred years before. He found a half completed church in Bayswater, an undeveloped area then on the fringes of London, and got it finished by July 1857. He later described his years as Father Superior with the Oblates as the happiest period of his life. Manning's enthusiasm and energy quickly led to Bayswater becoming a major centre of Catholic life in London. The initial group of seven priests grew to twenty within three years despite several of them dying of typhus. The number of communicants grew from 100 to 1,000. By 1865, when Manning left, the area had three Catholic churches, four convents, and eight Catholic schools. Manning's intense religious devotion marked all who knew him; as one Oblate remarked, he left:

'So holy a power upon our lives'.

Disputes between Wiseman and the Old Catholics

Unfortunately for Manning his hopes of a quiet life of pastoral service were to be spoiled because of disputes between Wiseman and the Old Catholics. When he came to England in 1851 Wiseman had tried to appease them by appointing George Errington, a leading Old Catholic and expert canon lawyer, as his coadjutor, with right of succession to the diocese. Unfortunately, this did not work, as Errington campaigned against Wiseman's policies almost from the start. To strengthen Wiseman's hand in 1857 Pius IX personally nominated Manning, to his great surprise, as Provost of the Westminster Chapter, to the outrage of the clergy there.

Errington attacks Manning's Oblates

This seems to have prompted Errington, with the support of most of the chapter, to attack Manning's Oblates. He first disputed their right to the original Church of St Mary of the Angels in Bayswater, and then turned upon the Oblates led by Vaughn who had been sent by Manning to teach at St Edmund's seminary Ware. Manning had written to Rome:

'I do not believe that seminaries will ever be what they ought to be in England unless they are directed by secular priests who have learned to live by rule, and can act with unity of mind and purpose'

The Pope dismisses Errington

Errington ordered Manning to submit the Rule of the Oblates to the Westminster Chapter. Manning, backed by Wiseman, refused. Errington then referred the matter to Rome, essentially suing Wiseman. In response Wiseman felt he had no alternative but to write to Rome in 1859 asking for Errington to be removed as coadjutor and his successor. The Pope decided that he had no alternative than to dismiss Errington. Pius IX publicly expressed his exasperation at these English priests who could not work together. 'The Italians think us all, Manning, Talbot, Newman, Ward etc. are a lot of queer, quarrelsome *Inglesi.*'

Wiseman comes to rely increasingly on Manning

In 1859 Wiseman suffered a heart attack, and from then on until the end of his life poor health led him to rely increasingly on Manning. He wrote to Cardinal Barnabó, Prefect of Propaganda:

'I do not hesitate to say that in all England there is not another priest who in double the time has done what Dr Manning has for the advantage of the Catholic Church.'

Now that Errington had been dismissed, the question of who would indeed succeed the ailing Wiseman became ever more apparent as the 1860s progressed. This is not to say that Wiseman was not always his own man; when, for example, Manning asked him to make the highly respected Ullathorne, Bishop of Birmingham, Wiseman's own coadjutor and successor, he was sternly rebuked.

Tense relations between Manning and Newman

The early 1860s also sadly saw increasingly tense relations between Manning and Newman. In 1861 Cardinal Wiseman set up a Catholic Academy where leading Catholic thinkers could discuss important issues of the day. However, Newman, notoriously oversensitive, thought he had been slighted for some reason and withdrew his name. Manning later wrote: 'From that day a divergence began between us'. Manning was the main force behind its creation, as throughout his life he passionately believed that the Church had to engage with modern society and be prepared to answer new questions that arose from scientific discoveries or political changes:

> 'We are in the modern world... and we must brace ourselves to lay hold of the world as it grapples with us and to meet it intellect to intellect, culture to culture, science to science.'

The champion of infallibility

Wiseman died on the 15 February 1865, leading to intense speculation about his successor. Manning wrote to Rome indicating that as a convert his own name should not be considered, and he again pushed for Ullathorne to take over. The Westminster Chapter in effect sent only one name- Errington. Pius IX was outraged, declaring this an 'insulto al Papa'.

The Pope hears a voice saying Manning's name

The Pope now came under intense lobbying pressure with the British Government pressing for Errington, while Propaganda advocated Ullathorne. Whilst praying for guidance Pius IX had a revelation:

> 'I found myself truly inspired to nominate him; and I will always believe to have heard a voice saying, "Put him there, Put him there!"'.

The English Church rallied around its new Archbishop

'Him' was of course Manning. When the official letter from Propaganda reached him on 8 May he was found praying before the Blessed Sacrament in the Oratory church. For once Manning's iron emotional control had given way; he had been crying. Propaganda had been worried that Manning's appointment could split the Church but to Manning's surprise and joy the English Church rallied round its new Archbishop.

The struggle for souls seen in Manning's face

Before his consecration Manning went on a week's retreat with the Passionists at Highgate. Whilst looking down on London from Highgate Hill he wrote:

'When I look down upon London from this garden and know that there are before me nearly three million of men of whom only 200,000 are nominally in the Faith... To go down into the fire and into the water to save souls, and to be wounded by them- all this I look for... I see it (the struggle) in my face'

Indeed, at his consecration at the pro-Cathedral of Mary Moorfields on the 8th June 1865 the marks of deep suffering were visible on his face. In his youth Manning had been regarded as one of the most handsome men in England; from now on the cumulative effect of intense austerity and superhuman spiritual discipline made his face increasingly emaciated.

People as a priority

The new Archbishop immediately showed his priorities. The leading Catholics of the day had raised £16,000 to build a new cathedral as a memorial to Wiseman, a huge sum in those days when the ordinary worker earned £30 a year. Manning disappointed them by using the money instead to build schools and train priests, arguing:

> 'Could I leave 20,000 children without education and drain my friends and my flock to pile up stones and brick?'

Attention on the international Church

However, the next few years were to see him spend much of his attention on the international Church. The Middle Ages had left Italy and Germany divided into a large number of small states, with the Papacy controlling the area around Rome. However, by the middle of the nineteenth century the forces of nationalism were growing. In 1861 the Kingdom of Savoy conquered the rest of the country, creating the Kingdom of Italy. Under the slogan, 'A free church in a free state', it confiscated Catholic property and restricted the Church's activities throughout Italy.

At the same time Bismarck used the Prussian army to occupy the other German states, proclaiming the creation of a new German Empire, or Second Reich, in 1871. Bismarck also launched a massive attack on the Catholic Church in the new Germany under the name of the *Kulturkampf*, or 'struggle for culture'. It was designed to assert the State's authority over the Church and reduce its influence; 1800 priests and most of the bishops were thrown into prison.

The 'new Biblical Criticism'

At the same time, another different threat was also coming from Germany. In the early 1800s the German Protestant theologian Schleiermacher developed his 'new Biblical criticism'. This attacked the traditional understanding of both the Bible and the Creeds, calling for a much more liberal church. From the 1850s onward German Catholic scholars such as Döllinger advocated many of Schleiermacher's ideas, with support from liberal Catholics in England such as Acton. In response Pius IX responded by issuing the *Syllabus of Errors* in 1864 condemning the chief errors of the age: 'progress, liberalism, and modern civilization'.

The Pope calls a General Council of the Church

The Pope decided to call a General Council of the Church, which opened in December 1869 to strengthen the Church from these two threats. The aim was to formally agree that, in principle and in certain circumstances, the Pope's teaching was infallible. Virtually all Catholic theologians agreed with this teaching, but many were concerned that publicly declaring it now could stir up further trouble for the Church. Since they thought the time was not right they were called 'inopportunists'.

Manning was the 'chief whip' of the 'infallibilist' party

Manning was the 'chief whip' of the 'infallibilist' party, not just because he thought that it was a useful supplement to ultramontanism against the encroachment of State power. To him it was much more than that, as infallibility lay at the basis of his personal faith. I noted earlier that throughout his early life he was seeking the 'rule of faith'; he became a Catholic because he became convinced that only the Catholic Church had the certain means of turning divine revelation into infallible teaching. In 1865 he wrote in his journal:

'When I was in a system of compromise I tried to meditate, reconcile and unite together those who differed. When I entered a system which, being divine, is definite and uncompromising, I threw myself with my whole soul and strength into its mind, will, and action.'

Manning used all of his formidable political skills to ensure that the Council agreed Papal infallibility. He relentlessly lobbied the assembled bishops, and took charge of the key Committee, *Deputation de Fide*, so that it was dominated by infallibilist supporters. Manning also made full use of his renowned oratorical powers, giving the keynote speech, in Italian, for two hours on 25 May 1870. He pointed out that:

'Papal infallibility is Catholic doctrine of divine faith, and all are already obliged to hold it… It is not an open theological opinion, but a doctrine contained in the divine revelation. Does anybody here doubt the doctrine?'

Manning's astonishing prescience

Manning also fervently believed that the Christian faith was fading from Europe, and that its absence would open the road to totalitarian dictatorship where men would worship their leaders, just as ancient Romans had worshipped Caesar. As he wrote to Gladstone:

'Of this I am sure as of the motion of the earth. My belief is that faith is gone from society as such; morals are going, and politics will end in the paralysis of the governing power. The end of this must be anarchy or despotism. I have been a fearless Radical all my life; and am not afraid of popular legislation, but legislation without principles is in strict sense anarchy. My belief is that Society without Christianity is the Commune (Communist dictatorship). What hope can you give me?'

These warnings were made nearly fifty years before the Russian Revolution, and sixty before Hitler took power, and show Manning's astonishing prescience. This was a time when it was almost universally accepted that human life was now in a period of unending improvement in economic and social affairs; indeed, belief in 'progress' was a characteristic of the Victorian period. Manning saw further. In Norman's words:

'He had an almost apocalyptic sense that the civilized world, for so long sustained by Christianity, was sliding into chaos; a sense that some great catastrophe for humanity was impending. Catholic unity, centralized in the papacy, was the only means, he believed, for Christendom to survive.[11]

Using his oratorical skills and fears for the future to persuade

He also used his oratorical skills and fears for the future to persuade the Council. One Bishop noted:

'Archbishop Manning, by his vehement and vivid forecasts of the evils which threatened us, made my hair stand on end. But there was a great deal of force in his arguments. Our opposition to the opportuneness of the definition was confined more or less to historical or theoretical objections; we gave little or no practical view of things which Manning insisted upon, to the coming events in the political order, wars and revolutions which he predicted with such terrible earnestness…We were, perhaps, more of the theologians; he more of an ecclesiastical statesman.'

On 18 July the definition was approved by 433 votes in favour and 2 against. The timing could not have been more dramatic. A day later France declared war on Germany, and the French troops who had been protecting Rome were withdrawn. The Council had to be abandoned as Italian forces occupied the city.

Infallibility and its relevancy

I suspect that some Catholics may regard this subject as archaic and irrelevant. The *Catechism of the Catholic Church* (1994) says otherwise:

> '(S889) In order to preserve the Church in the purity of the faith handed on by the apostles, Christ who is the Truth willed to confer on her a share in his own infallibility. By a "supernatural sense of faith" the People of God, under the guidance of the Church's living Magisterium, "unfailingly adheres to this faith". (S890) … It is the Magisterium's task to preserve God's people from deviations and defections and to guarantee them the objective possibility of professing the true faith without error... To fulfil this service, Christ endowed the Church's shepherds with the charism of infallibility in matters of faith and morals.'[12]

People sometimes suggest that the Second Vatican Council marked a huge change in the nature of the Church away from the model presented at the first

Vatican Council. I would like to respond to such ideas by quoting from one of the definitive documents of the Second Vatican Council, *Lumen Gentium- the Dogmatic Constitution on the Church. Lumen Gentium* states:

> 'This infallibility with which the divine Redeemer wills His Church to be endowed in defining a doctrine of faith and morals extends as far as and extends the deposit of divine revelation, which must be religiously guarded and faithfully expounded. This is the infallibility which the Roman Pontiff, the head of the college of bishops, enjoys in virtue of all office, when, as the supreme shepherd and teacher of all the faithful, who confirms his brethren in their faith (cf Lk. 22:32), he proclaims by a definitive act some doctrine of faith or morals.'[13]

The Father of Catholic Social Teaching

When he returned from the Vatican Council Manning gave a series of six lectures, published under the title *The Fourfold Sovereignty of God*.[14] It describes society as:

'More than a collection of individuals... (It is) united, ordered, and organized by an intrinsic law of their nature. For when God made man, He made society... society springs out of the creation of man because from man comes the family, and from the family comes the people, and from the people comes the state.'

Christianity leading to morality

People today in their ignorance often accuse Christianity of being a negative force. Manning knew that the opposite is true, i.e. that it was Christianity which led to a society based upon morality rather than brute force. He was thinking particularly of Ancient Rome, a great civilization that was built upon a massive-slave state terrorised by the threat of torture and crucifixion. When this military superpower imploded in the fifth century, Europe collapsed into the chaos of the Dark Ages, before a new civilization based upon Christian principles emerged:

'What has the world, then, gained by the sovereignty of Jesus Christ? The extinction of slavery- and let any man weigh what those words mean, remembering what slavery was in the ancient world. Secondly the sanctification of Christian households by the laws of marriage and the laws of domestic purity... Again, a quality unknown before Christianity came on earth- unknown altogether in the heathen world- was infused into the hearts of men, that is charity- a tenderness, and a human sympathy of man for man. It is a fact too well known to dwell upon that in the heathen world not a hospital was to be found. Even in its most advanced civilization before Christianity the sick died without mercy.'

He criticised the secular idea of progress

He criticised the secular idea of progress which dominated thinking in the nineteenth century, arguing that 'progress signifies an advance in the order of perfection'. Manning also noted that British politicians were already talking of 'Religious Difficulties', which they claimed were preventing children being educated together in a common way, and warned posterity that this was only the beginning of attacks on the Church. One hundred and forty years later, when employees are sacked for daring to wear a cross, and Catholic adoption agencies are forcibly closed by the State, we can only and sadly admire his percipience:

'Modern civilization is making progress, it is true; but what will it progress to? To the utter and entire rejection of Christianity; to the abolition of the "religious difficulty" from legislation, from education, and from domestic life; to the relegating and banishing of religion from all public life to the individual conscience and private life of man...
...There is yet a time of stillness and indifference.' Liberalism is a twilight state in which all errors are softened, in which no persecution for religion will be countenanced. It is the stillness before the storm.'

A public debate with Gladstone on the State

Manning's views led him to a public debate with Gladstone about the encroaching power of the State, but again his pessimism and prescience has been vindicated by history. As one scholar notes:

'"The conflict now raging", Manning maintained, was nothing less than one, "between Christianity and Anti-Christianity"...(it) would be fought out over issues having to do with education, laws concerning marriage and family, public and private morality'.[15]

A 'Mosaic Radical'

Manning described himself as a 'Mosaic Radical', i.e. his vision was based upon the moral law handed down to Moses, i.e. the Ten Commandments. Sheridan Gilley has highlighted Manning's prophetic vision:

'It was however, the apocalyptic element in Manning's vision which made him a prophet....responding to the drama of a world which was being transformed... Manning looked into two great neighbouring abysses, the abyss of unbelief and the abyss of revolution from below, and saw European society rushing towards them.'[16]

Thirty years after Manning's death Hilaire Belloc reminisced:

'The profound thing which Cardinal Manning said to me was this: "all human conflict is ultimately theological".'

Education of the poor

Throughout his life Manning was concerned about the education of the poor. One of his top priorities when he became Archbishop was establishing primary schools for the poor of the diocese. He was particularly concerned about the way poor orphan Irish children, detained in workhouses, were being brought up in ignorance of the Faith, and he used his influence with Gladstone to have an amendment to the Poor Law passed which obliged workhouses to release them if requested. These children were not then left alone on the streets. The Archbishop founded Catholic industrial schools where children lived and learnt a trade along with the Faith; a government inspector found that an industrial school founded by Manning at Ilford was the best in the country. In his Lenten Pastoral of 1890, he looked back on this work. By 1889 the Westminster diocese had 18,912 Catholics in junior schools compared with 11,000 in 1865. Over 10,000 children had been rescued from workhouses with 4,500 of these trained at industrial schools. In Gray's words:

'Manning's determination to ensure that poor children should not be lost to the Faith, shows him at his best, his concern for the unfortunate and his pastoral zeal combining with his great administrative ability... He was easily the most accomplished and beneficent man of affairs the Church has possessed in England since the Reformation.'[17]

Foster's 1870 Education Act created new 'Board' schools completely funded by the government, deliberate policy to try and push the church schools out of existence. By 1884 financial pressures had forced more the 1,000 voluntary schools to close, although intense effort kept all of the Catholic schools open. Their survival was only due to Manning's shrewdness in encouraging Religious Orders, particularly nuns, to come forward as unpaid teachers.

'How Shall Catholics vote at the coming Parliamentary Election?'

When in 1885 the Liberal Joseph Chamberlain announced plans for local boards to take over the running of voluntary schools, the Cardinal felt that this attack on Catholic schools forced the Church to abandon its normal rule of political neutrality, and published an article, *'How Shall Catholics vote at the coming Parliamentary Election?'* opposing the Liberals, who lost. Lord Salisbury's new Conservative government appointed a Commission led by Lord Cross to look at the working of the 1870 Education Act, with Manning the 'dominant figure' on it.[18] The Cross Commission recommended that voluntary schools should receive the same level of aid as the board schools, implemented by the 1902 Education Act.

A Catholic University

In 1872 Manning set up a Catholic university in London. The policy of the Catholic Church at the time was strongly against young Catholics going to non-Catholic universities. The new university was designed to provide an attractive and theologically sound alternative, as Manning worried:

'Count De Maistre has said that history since the Reformation has been a conspiracy against the Catholic Church. We may say that philosophy since Descartes has to a wider extent than suspected joined in the conspiracy. And yet these are essentially the history and philosophy delivered at the English Universities. '

Unfortunately the new university was badly run and inadequately funded, and forced to close after a few years.

Made a cardinal and proposed for the papacy

In 1875 Pius IX made Manning a cardinal, and when he died in 1878 Manning's was one of the names put forward as his replacement, the first time since the Middle Ages that an Englishman had been so honoured. However he himself strongly argued that the Church needed another Italian Pope, and Leo XIII was elected.

Calling for a change of policy in Ireland

Manning was unusual for an English Roman Catholic leader in shaping English attitudes to Ireland, at that time part of the British Empire. The Irish countryside seethed with unrest following the horrors of the Irish Famine from 1847 onwards, when over one and a quarter million people, a quarter of the population, are estimated to have died from hunger. The English authorities did little to help. Sir Charles Trevelyan, the senior civil servant responsible for funding relief argued in his 1848 book, *The Irish Crisis*, that the Famine was simply the inevitable result of Irish over breeding, as Malthus had predicted. The renowned classics scholar Benjamin Jowett, master of Balliol College Oxford, wrote:

> 'I have always felt a certain horror of political economists since I heard one of them say that he feared that the Famine of 1848 in Ireland would not kill more than a million people, and that scarcely enough to do much good.'

The Poor Law Act of 1847 incorporated the 'Gregory Provision', which denied poor relief of any kind to anyone in Ireland who possessed more than a quarter acre of land. The Poor Law Commission's aim was make farming more efficient by encouraging land clearance and emigration:

'The two great deficiencies in Ireland are want of capital, and want of industry. By destroying small tenancies you obtain both.'[19]

Starving Irish Catholic peasants saw no reason to pay rents to what they felt to be grasping absentee, Protestant English landlords. Secret societies threatened rent collectors, maimed animals, and burned down buildings owned by the State. The British government's initial response to this unrest was through repression, but this only controlled and did not solve the problem. From the 1880s onwards Parnell founded the Land League who pushed for land reform and some kind of home rule.

Manning takes up the Irish claim

Only one prominent English figure called for a change of policy in Ireland- Cardinal Manning. In 1868 he published *The Letter to Earl Grey*, arguing that there had to be religious equality, i.e. the Disestablishment of the Church of Ireland and the abolition of the infamous land laws which gave tenants no protection against arbitrary eviction or draconian rent increases. He took up the Irish claim of the 'three Fs': Fair rents, Fixity of tenure, and Free Sale. The *Quarterly Review* had previously declared that: 'It has been the pleasure of Ireland to pass upon itself a sentence of perpetual poverty'. *The Letter to Earl Grey* pulled no punches:

'Did Ireland suicidally strip itself of all its lands; reduce itself to mud-cabins, potato diet, and evictions, fever and famine? Who checked its agriculture, its cattle trade, its fisheries, and its manufactures by Acts of Parliament? If poverty was ever inflicted by one nation on another, it has been inflicted on Ireland by England.'

The Cardinal's lobbying led to Gladstone's Land Acts of 1870 and 1881 fulfilling most of Manning's proposals. He also adopted the controversial position of public support for the Land League, although never for violent action, and he persuaded the Pope to reject the British government's request to condemn it. In 1881 an Irish priest visited Manning:

'When dinner was over and the visit to the Blessed Sacrament, the Cardinal drew me into the corridor and said, "Oh, I fear very link of affection between the two countries is broken." "Yes", I said, "all but one". "What is that?" said the Cardinal. "Our love for you", said I. I shall never forget how he looked me through when he answered: "Do you mean that?" I said:" You are the last man in England to whom I would say that if I did not believe it to be true" And the dear old man burst into tears. After a bit, almost under his breath: "It is what I have prayed for, it is what I have prayed for". I don't think many men have seen Manning cry.'

Practical ecumenism

The Victorians had a strong tendency to ignore the dark underworld of their time, but Manning always reached out to the despised. In the 1870s he campaigned for better conditions in prisons, and obtained the right for them to have Catholic chaplains. He was also not afraid to question Victorian hypocrisy against women. In Victorian London priests and doctors would go into slums that police were afraid to enter. The aged Cardinal advised them:

> 'Give yourself to London. It is the abomination of desolation. No one knows the depths of the sufferings of the women, save the doctor and the priest.'

Raising the age of responsibility

In the mid 1880s the Cardinal, along with Bramwell Booth, the leader of the Salvation Army, and the newspaper editor W.T. Stead shocked polite society with their revelations of widespread child sex trafficking in London. As a result the age of responsibility for sexual intercourse was raised from thirteen to sixteen in order to make it easier to convict the traffickers. Bramwell Booth said of Manning:

> 'I do not think that outside the Salvation Army I ever met a man who more uncompromisingly brought his

religion into everything he touched, into everything he wrote, into everything he planned. He did it with the most exquisite tact, and without the slightest suggestion of putting himself forward, but he did it.'

Campaigning to prohibit the opium trade

As one scholar notes: 'no one could describe Manning as an ecumenist before his time, and he was dismissive of movements for Church Reunion.'[20] However, he had a strong willingness to work with other churches on social issues. For example together with Anglican and Methodist leaders he campaigned to prohibit the opium trade in the British Empire.[21]

Expressing admiration for John Wesley

The Cardinal also shocked and surprised many Catholics by expressing his admiration for John Wesley: 'If it had not been for the teaching of John Wesley, no man can tell how deep in degradation England would have sunk.' Probably Manning's greatest sympathy with Wesley came in the field of alcohol. Wesley had not been against wine as such, but was wary of its social impact, i.e. he had objected to the way that the tavern-keepers of his day were exploiting the weakness of the poor to enrich themselves, whilst driving the poor deeper into penury. Manning took the temperance pledge himself in 1872, and he founded the Catholic League of the Cross.

Although by 1876 58,000 people had joined it, both this campaign, and Manning's collaboration with other churches was not popular with the rest of the hierarchy, as Gilley has observed:

'In the 1870s Manning's social activism…placed the Catholic Church at the forefront of the movement for social and political reform. Conservative Catholics shuddered when Manning appeared on a largely Protestant platform to endorse the Primitive Methodist Joseph Arch's Agricultural Union, when he denounced the programs against Russian Jews, when he applauded the social activism of the Salvation Army'[22]

Popular with the working classes

The Cardinal was undeterred by this sniping. In 1872 he supported the creation of a trade union for agricultural workers. (He had fought for better conditions for country labourers since ministering to them in Sussex forty years earlier.) In 1884 he served on the Royal Commission led by Dilke to inquire into the housing of the working classes. This gave great encouragement to the newly created London County Council in building cheap social housing. Owen Chadwick admitted:

'With the working classes he was …the most popular clergyman in England.'[23]

In the nineteenth century the lives of most working people was a combination of hard toil and little reward. Historians have called it 'the bleak age'. No one of importance really challenged the free-market or 'laissez-faire' orthodoxy of the day until Cardinal Manning went to the Leeds Mechanics Institute in January 1874 to lecture on *The Dignity and Rights of Labour*.[24] The speech begins by noting that industrialists were fond of quoting Thessalonians 2 iii.10, 'If a man will not work, neither will he eat', but that they ignored Luke x. 7, 'the labourer is worthy of his hire'.

'The Dignity and Rights of Labour'

Manning pointed out that the hard lives of the workers was a political risk as it was a fertile breeding ground for extreme politics. He made certain key recommendations: employers should not pay starvation wages which turned the worker into a wage-slave, for a free society demanded that labour should have some choice where and how it worked, and a starving man had none. He asked that recognition should be given to associations of working men, and pointed out the work of mutual support which had been carried out by the medieval guilds. Lastly, he requested some consideration for the family, pointing out how families of 14 or 15 were huddled together in one room, usually in appalling sanitary conditions. Nevertheless, despite his advocacy for the poor, he was keen to warn against emerging Marxist ideas which were then gaining currency:

'When I see the word proletariat in a book, I suspect the book at once.'

Manning's influence on the great social encyclical *Rerum Novarum*

All these ideas, the need for decent wages, the right to form trade unions, and the family as the basis of society are the major themes running through the great social encyclical *Rerum Novarum* issued by Pope Leo XIII in May 1891. Indeed, Manning had a profound influence on that document. When the Latin original was produced Manning was sent a copy with a request that he should be the official translator into English. The Pope added that he was 'grateful for the influential communications' he had received from the English Cardinal prior to writing it. Archbishop Walsh wrote to Manning from Rome that he 'traced your Eminence's influence in this as in many other things'. McClelland notes that:

'Manning was always listened to with awe at Rome because of his great record in the shaping of Church policy and because of his particular interests in the field of Labour-Church relations.'[26]

In July 1891 Manning wrote a review of *Rerum Novarum* for the *Dublin Review*. His conclusion can be seen as a good justification of Catholic social teaching:

'For a century the Civil Powers in almost all the Christian world have been separating themselves from the Church, claiming and glorifying in their separation. They have set up the State as a purely lay and secular society, and have thrust the Church from them. And now of a sudden they find that the millions of the world sympathise with the Church, which has compassion on the multitude, rather than with the State, or the plutocracy which has weighed so heavily upon them.'

The similarity of thought and tone with the encyclical can be seen from the passage from *Rerum Novarum* below:

'By degrees it has come to pass that Working Men have been given over, isolated and defenceless, to the callousness of employers and the greed of unrestrained competition. The evil has been increased by rapacious Usury... And to this must be added the custom of working by contract, and the concentration of so many branches of trade in the hands of a few individuals, so that a small number of very rich men have been able to lay upon the masses of the poor a yoke little better than slavery itself.'[27]

His life's work for the people

In my opinion Manning may truly be described as the 'father of Catholic Social Teaching'. Personally, I am also pleased that he lived just long enough to see a Papal encyclical endorsing his crusades for social justice. Alan McClelland agrees:

'The old man could be forgiven, perhaps, for rejoicing that *Rerum Novarum* had set the final seal of approval upon his life's work for the people, and in so doing, had confounded his critics.'[28]

Manning's role in the Great Dock Strike

Manning's role in ending the great Dock Strike of 1889 brought him international recognition. This strike was a major event in economic history as it was the first time that a mass union had successfully organised a major strike. It was recognised as such at the time:

'The dock strike took the world by surprise; it was something quite new, upsetting all men's calculations'.

At this time relatively unskilled workers such as dockers were very much the bottom of the pile. They were casual labourers who queued up twice a day in the 'call-on' system to be hired by the hour. They were paid 5d (2.1p) an hour; often many of the men who had waited for hours got no work and hence no money for them or their families. The final straw that led to the strike breaking out was the decision by the West India Docks company in the summer of 1889 to cut the 'plus money', the small bonus paid to dock crews for rapid completion of the work. On the 14th August 1889 the dock workers walked out, demanding a minimum work shift of four hours and an increase in wages to 6d an hour, called 'the dockers' tanner'. Although there was a union led by Ben Tillet, it was small and had minimal resources; the dock owners believed that financial pressures would soon force them back to work.

However to general surprise other workers in the Port of London such as the stevedores and firemen joined the strike; by 27 August there was in effect a general strike in the docks, with 130,000 men. Of course the poorly paid dockers had no savings, and hunger would have soon ended the strike had it not been for a wave of support throughout the East End, with churches establishing soup kitchens, and for financial support arriving from abroad, especially Australia. The strikers were keenly aware of the legal background, and while there was picketing, it was peaceful with no recorded intimidation.

By the beginning of September the strike was paralysing Victorian London. The dock owners threatened to import workers from the Continent to break the strike. The government decided that a means had to be found to settle it, and a Committee of Conciliation was established on the 5th September at the Mansion House, led by the Lord Mayor, representatives of the dock owners, and Cardinal Manning. The latter wrote:

'I became certain that fresh efforts were about to be made to bring labourers from a distance....which would lead to violent resistance, probably to bloodshed. Finding that no other mediation acceptable to the combatants appeared to be available, I resolved to offer my humble services with the endeavour to bring them together'.

The Committee then met with the dockers' leaders Ben Tillett and Tom Burns. However, agreement over the 'dockers' tanner' could not be reached. Negotiations almost collapsed, and only Manning's iron will, and his warnings of potential bloodshed, kept the Committee intact. He then single-handedly negotiated with both the dockers and the owners. For four days over the following weekend the 81 year Cardinal pressed both sides to come to an agreement. Finally, he got the dockers' leaders to agree that the 6d rate could come into force on the 1st November rather than immediately. He then spent several more days persuading the dock owners to accept, which they finally did. Manning later stated: 'I never in my life preached to so impenitent a congregation'. *The Morning Post* captured the general mood:

'The result is due in a great measure to the individual efforts of Cardinal Manning, who has laboured assiduously in spite of his eighty-one years.'

'The Eternal Priesthood'

In 1883 Manning wrote his greatest spiritual work; a practical guide to priestly ministry entitled *The Eternal Priesthood*.[29] Norman rates the book highly:

'His intellectual interests were wide, however, and he wrote with a deceptive simplicity a number of short works which had great spiritual depth, especially *The Eternal Priesthood*.[30]

The book consists of twenty-two chapters with titles like 'the nature of priesthood' or 'the priest's dangers', and it sets out his high vision of priestly vocation:

'The offering of the Body and Blood of Christ requires of the priest a spirit of self-sacrifice and of self-oblation without reserve. The obligation of charity, which binds all Christians, when the need may arise, to lay down their lives for the brethren, and pastors to lay down their life for the sheep, is in an especial way laid upon every priest in their self-oblation of the Holy Mass, which is the Sacrifice of Jesus Christ… Albertus Magnus and S Thomas have said truly that no greater power or dignity of consecrating the Body of Christ was ever bestowed on man; and no greater sanctity or perfection can be conceived than the sanctity and perfection required for so divine an action in the priest'.

Nevertheless, although *The Eternal Priesthood* is meant to be a practical guide, at times the author becomes almost poetical in his exultation of the powers, and huge responsibility, of the priesthood:

'The priest has also jurisdiction over the mystical body of Christ... What can be more formidable than to stand between the living and the dead, charged with the priestly office, to give account for the souls committed to our trust? The Fathers call it an office which angels fear to bear.'

Sheridan Gilley notes that the book was highly influential:

'Manning's most influential work was *The Eternal Priesthood*, which is not only notable for its high Ultramontane doctrine of the authority of the priest, but for its uncompromising otherworldly demand that the priest live a life of utter dedication and holy poverty like his Lord.'[31]

Manning's influence on the Church

The Cardinal's influence on those who knew him was long lasting- over fifty years in the case of Hilaire Belloc, whose political and social thought was explicitly based upon Manning's.

'Manning did seem to me much the greatest Englishman of his time. He was certainly the greatest of all that band, small but immensely significant, who, in the Victorian period, so rose above their fellows.[32]

The case of Virginia Crawford is worth noting. In the early 1880s Manning became friends with the leading Liberal minister Sir Charles Dilke. However in late 1885 Dilke's political career was destroyed when he was accused by a Mr Crawford of adultery with his wife Virginia. Virginia was divorced and became a social outcast. Distraught, she sought counsel from the Cardinal, and on February 4 1889 she was received into the Catholic Church. The rest of her life until her death in 1948 was devoted to Manning's causes:

'On behalf of the Catholic emigration Society, she visited the Canadian settlements of English and Irish children. She was one of the pioneers of the Catholic

Social Guild, a society formed to make known Catholic social teaching, especially the encyclical *Rerum Novarum*... She could never stop talking about Manning.'[33]

Cardinal Manning died on the morning of the 14th January 1892. His successor Herbert Vaughn had been embarrassed by Manning's social campaigns and this work was abandoned. Yet Manning's achievements were never entirely forgotten. In 1950 the English Bishops commissioned a major volume of essays to commemorate the restoration of the hierarchy in 1850. The first essay by Fr Philip Hughes has much on Manning:

'Alas, the leader of genius formed no school, left no Eliseus (Elisha) to catch his mantle as he sped from earth. But the memory of his universal sympathies, of his generous indignation, of his virile public courage remained to animate a younger generation...and to strengthen the outspoken sympathies of the great cardinal of the war years, Arthur Hinsley. Nor are the echoes yet silent of Manning's mighty veracity.[34]

Indeed, Hinsley, who was Archbishop of Westminster from 1935-1943, campaigned for the poor during the Great Depression of the 1930s just as Manning had done in his time. As the *Daily Herald* wrote: 'Not since Manning has Britain had a Cardinal who so closely identified himself with the lives of the common people'.

In 1939 Cardinal Hinsley hosted a celebratory dinner to mark the fiftieth anniversary of the Dock Strike, with organizer Tom Burns present. This dinner was recorded by a promising young priest called John Heenan, who in his turn became Archbishop of Westminster from 1963-1975.[35] Three Cardinals, three workers for the common good of England.

The public's depth of affection

Immediately after the Cardinal's death the magazine *Merry England*, published a series of 'Memorials' about him that show the public's massive depth of affection for a warmly loved figure. I think that English Catholicism was traumatised when Purcell's apparently authoritative but in truth distorted and biased biography appeared three years later. It appeared to show that the beloved Cardinal was in fact a cold and ruthless figure consumed by ambition.

It is my hope that this brief biography will help set the matter straight, and restore Henry Manning to his rightful place, worthy of veneration as one of the greatest leaders of English Catholicism. Let me end however with some words of Manning himself, 'The Priest's Rewards', from *The Eternal Priesthood:*

'If the pastoral office is to be loved everywhere, it is to be loved especially in England. We are the pastors of the poor, and poor ourselves, separate from courts and honours, slighted and set aside in apostolic liberty, in faith and work independent of all human authority, closely and vitally united with the See of Peter and with the church throughout the world: heirs of the Martyrs, saints, Confessors of every age, from St. Augustine to this day'.

Endnotes

[1] *'Rerum Novarum* - The Condition of Labor', reproduced in *The Social Teachings of the Church*, ed Anne Freemantle, Mentor-Omega, New York, New York, USA 1963.

[2] Robert Gray, *Cardinal Manning- A Biography*, Weidenfeld and Nicholson, London 1985.

[3] Gray, *op cit.*

[4] David Newsome, *The Convert Cardinals- Newman and Manning*, John Murray London 1993.

[5] *The Convert Cardinals - op cit.*

[6] Gray, *op cit.*

[7] James Pereiro, quoted in 'Caroline, the lost love of the Cardinal', *The Church Times*, 9 March 2009.

[8] James Pereiro, *Cardinal Manning: An Intellectual Biography*, the Clarendon Press, Oxford, 1998.

[9] Sheridan Gilley, 'The Roman Catholic Church in England, 1780-1940', in *A History of Religion in Britain,* Ed S. Gilley and W.J. Shiels, Blackwell, Oxford 1994.

[10] Edward Norman - *Roman Catholicism in England- from the Elizabethan Settlement to the Second Vatican Council*, Oxford University Press 1985.

[11] Norman - *op cit.*

[12] *Cathechism of the Catholic Church*, English Translation Geoffrey Chapman, London 1994.

[13] *The Documents of Vatican II - the meaning of the Ecumenical Council*, translated from the Latin, Geoffrey Chapman, London-Dublin 1966.

[14] H.E. Manning, *The Fourfold Sovereignty of God*, Burns & Oates, London, 1871.

[15] Jeffrey von Arx SJ, 'Archbishop Manning and the Kulturkampf', *Recusant History* Vol 21 No2 October 1992.

[16] Sheridan Gilley, 'Manning and Chesterton', *The Chesterton Review,* Vol XVIII No 4 November 1992.

[17] Gray *op cit.*

[18] V.A McClelland, *Cardinal Manning - his public life and influence 1865-1892*, Oxford University Press 1962.

[19] Quoted in R. Foster, *Modern Ireland 1600-1972*, Penguin London 1989.

[20] David Newsome, 'Cardinal Manning and his Influence on the Church and Nation', *Recusant History* Vol 21 No2 October 1992.

[21] John Crangle, 'Cardinal Manning's Role in the Suppression of the British Opium Trade', *London Recusant*, Vol 6 1976.

[22] Gilley 'The Roman Catholic Church in England, *op cit.*

[23] Owen Chadwick *The Victorian Church, Part 2, 1860-1901*, A&C Black, London 1970.

[24] H.E. Manning, 'The Dignity and Rights of Labour', in *The Writings of Cardinal Manning on Social Problems*, Burns Oates and Washbourne London 1934.

[25] *Rerum Novarum op cit.*

[26] McClelland, *Cardinal Manning op cit.*

[27] *Rerum Novarum, op cit.*

[28] V McClelland, 'Manning's Work for Social Justice', *The Chesterton Review*, Vol XVIII No 4 November 1992.

[29] H.E. Manning, *The Eternal Priesthood,* Burns Oates, London 1883.

[30] Norman *op cit.*

[31] Gilley 'The Roman Catholic Church in England' *op cit.*

[32] Hilaire Belloc, *The Cruise of the Nona,* Constable & Co, London 1925.

[33] Francis Bywater, 'Cardinal Manning and the Dilke Divorce Case', *The Chesterton Review*, Vol XVIII No 4 November 1992.

[34] Philip Hughes, 'The Coming Century', in G.A.Beck (Ed), *The English Catholics 1850-1950,* Burns Oates London 1950.

[35] J C Heenan, *Cardinal Hinsley,* Burns Oates & Washbourne, London 1944.

Catholic Social Teaching
A Way In

'The Common Good', 'option for the poor' 'subsidiarity'-concepts like these have become part of the currency of Catholic teaching, but what do they mean? What are their foundations in scripture and tradition which make them distinctively Catholic?

This book examines key aspects of human social relations such as the family, the state and civil society, the world of work and justice. It explains in clear language how a conscience informed by divine revelation brings out the true human vocation to love of God and neighbour. The author highlights the particular contribution of Pope John Paul II and Pope Benedict XVI.

In an increasingly materialist, individualist and utilitarian world this book opens up a rich heritage of teaching and reflection.

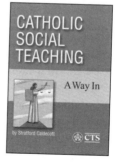

CATHOLIC SOCIAL TEACHING

A Way In

by Stratford Caldecott

CTS

ISBN: 978 1 86082 116 5

CTS Code: Do 675

The Credit Crunch
Making moral sense of the financial crisis

The current financial crisis will affect all of us whether we are religious or not, but could adhering to some fundamental principles of Catholic Social Teaching have prevented the problem we now face or present us with a solution to ensure this doesn't happen again? Edward Hadas, author and financial journalist, analyses the reasons why the present disaster has occurred and makes serious proposals for a new more moral financial system.

Edward Hadas is Assistant Editor at *breakingviews.com*, a London-based internet financial commentary service. He is the author of *Human Goods, Economic Evils: A Moral Approach to the Dismal Science* (ISI Books, 2007). He is currently working on a book of Catholic Social Teaching.

ISBN: 978 1 86082 584 2

CTS Code: S 445

Democracy & Tyranny
The Catholic understanding of the state and politics

The Church's teaching authority has for some time now addressed the question of the better ordering of human societies, and which form of government best promotes human flourishing. Grounded in the Church's social doctrine, this booklet intends to clarify the central and defining features of the two commonly found forms of government: democracy, and its opposite, tyranny.

Thomas R. Rourke is a professor of politics at Clarion University in Pennsylvania. His previous books are, *A Conscience as Large as the World* (Rowman and Littlefield, 1997) and *A Theory of Personalism* (Lexington Books, 2005). He has also published articles in *Communio*.

ISBN: 978 1 86082 588 0

CTS Code: S 446